AESOP REFABLED

Eight short plays inspired by Aesop's Fables by
Nicole B. Adkins, Jeff Goode, Adam Hahn,
Samantha Macher, Liz Shannon Miller, Dominic Mishler,
Mike Rothschild and Dave Ulrich
SkyPilot Theatre Company Playwrights-in-Residence

www.youthplays.com
info@youthplays.com
424-703-5315

Aesop Refabled © 2012 Nicole B. Adkins, Jeff Goode, Adam Hahn, Samantha Macher, Liz Shannon Miller, Dominic Mishler, Mike Rothschild and Dave Ulrich
All rights reserved. ISBN 978-1-62088-161-3.

Caution: This play is fully protected under the copyright laws of the United States of America, Canada, the British Commonwealth and all other countries of the copyright union and is subject to royalty for all performances including but not limited to professional, amateur, charity and classroom whether admission is charged or presented free of charge.

Reservation of Rights: This play is the property of the authors and all rights for its use are strictly reserved and must be licensed by their representative, YouthPLAYS. This prohibition of unauthorized professional and amateur stage presentations extends also to motion pictures, recitation, lecturing, public reading, radio broadcasting, television, video and the rights of adaptation or translation into non-English languages.

Performance Licensing and Royalty Payments: Amateur and stock performance rights are administered exclusively by YouthPLAYS. No amateur, stock or educational theatre groups or individuals may perform this play without securing authorization and royalty arrangements in advance from YouthPLAYS. Required royalty fees for performing this play are available online at www.YouthPLAYS.com. Royalty fees are subject to change without notice. Required royalties must be paid each time this play is performed and may not be transferred to any other performance entity. All licensing requests and inquiries should be addressed to YouthPLAYS.

Author Credit: All groups or individuals receiving permission to produce this play must give the author(s) credit in any and all advertisements and publicity relating to the production of this play. The author's billing must appear directly below the title on a separate line with no other accompanying written matter. The name of the author(s) must be at least 50% as large as the title of the play. No person or entity may receive larger or more prominent credit than that which is given to the author(s) and the name of the author(s) may not be abbreviated or otherwise altered from the form in which it appears in this Play.

Publisher Attribution: All programs, advertisements, flyers or other printed material must include the following notice:
Produced by special arrangement with YouthPLAYS (www.youthplays.com).

Prohibition of Unauthorized Copying: Any unauthorized copying of this book or excerpts from this book, whether by photocopying, scanning, video recording or any other means, is strictly prohibited by law. This book may only be copied by licensed productions with the purchase of a photocopy license, or with explicit permission from YouthPLAYS.

Trade Marks, Public Figures & Musical Works: This play may contain references to brand names or public figures. All references are intended only as parody or other legal means of expression. This play may also contain suggestions for the performance of a musical work (either in part or in whole). YouthPLAYS has not obtained performing rights of these works unless explicitly noted. The direction of such works is only a playwright's suggestion, and the play producer should obtain such permissions on their own. The website for the U.S. copyright office is *http://www.copyright.gov*.

COPYRIGHT RULES TO REMEMBER

1. To produce this play, you must receive prior written permission from YouthPLAYS and pay the required royalty.

2. You must pay a royalty each time the play is performed in the presence of audience members outside of the cast and crew. Royalties are due whether or not admission is charged, whether or not the play is presented for profit, for charity or for educational purposes, or whether or not anyone associated with the production is being paid.

3. No changes, including cuts or additions, are permitted to the script without written prior permission from YouthPLAYS.

4. Do not copy this book or any part of it without written permission from YouthPLAYS.

5. Credit to the author and YouthPLAYS is required on all programs and other promotional items associated with this play's performance.

When you pay royalties, you are recognizing the hard work that went into creating the play and making a statement that a play is something of value. We think this is important, and we hope that everyone will do the right thing, thus allowing playwrights to generate income and continue to create wonderful new works for the stage.

Plays are owned by the playwrights who wrote them. Violating a playwright's copyright is a very serious matter and violates both United States and international copyright law. Infringement is punishable by actual damages and attorneys' fees, statutory damages of up to $150,000 per incident, and even possible criminal sanctions. **Infringement is theft. Don't do it.**

Have a question about copyright? Please contact us by email at info@youthplays.com or by phone at 424-703-5315. When in doubt, please ask.

PRODUCTION NOTES

Aesop Refabled is a collection of short stage plays inspired by the classic fables of Aesop.

The plays can be performed as individual pieces or grouped together in any combination to create a show of the desired length and performed under the title ***Aesop Refabled***.

The fables which inspired each play have been translated by the playwrights and included in this edition as optional material that can be used as part of classroom study or incorporated into a production. For example, a voiceover narration intoning the moral of the fable might be used as an introduction or a conclusion to each piece or shown as a projection above the stage.

PRODUCTION HISTORY

Aesop Refabled was conceived and developed by Nicole B. Adkins in collaboration with SkyPilot Theatre Company in Los Angeles under founding artistic director Bob Rusch and written by members of the company's Playwrights Wing. It was first performed as part of SkyPilot's New Play Reading Series on August 21, 2011, with the following cast:

Mackenzie English, Jude Evans, Brett Fleisher, Eric Curtis Johnson, Monica Lawson and Niki Nowak.

The plays were workshopped with Determined to Succeed, an educational non-profit organization in Los Angeles on January 14, 2012, with the following cast:

Kareem Cervantes, Mackenzie English, Eric Curtis Johnson, Samantha Macher and Niki Nowak.

Special thanks to Determined to Succeed students Jasmine Logan, Omeka Ikegbu, Sara Elmourabit, Christopher Madrigal, Jacqueline Trejo, Elizabeth DeLeon, Julieta Valencia, Diana Ovalle, Diana Pena, and Mario Hernandez for their invaluable insights, questions, and responses during script development.

Aesop Refabled premiered as part of SkyPilot Theatre Company's One-Act Series on May 14, 2012, under the direction of Lois Weiss; technical direction and stage management by Heidi Hostetler; with the following cast:

Katie Apicella, Kareem Cervantes, Kelly Goodman, Tom Kremer, Ellen Rae Littman, Jen Michaels, Brett Newton, Niki Nowak, Christopher Palle, Bart Petty, Ethan Zachery Scott

LIST OF PLAYS

Andy and Chrys by Nicole B. Adkins
Cheer Squad by Jeff Goode
The Raven and the Swan by Dave Ulrich
The Student and the Mathematician by Adam Hahn
Can't Forget by Liz Shannon Miller
The Lion and the Boar by Mike Rothschild
Bat, Birds, and Beasts by Dominic Mishler
The Warrior's Belt by Samantha Macher

ANDY AND CHRYS
by Nicole B. Adkins

after Aesop's fable The Ant and the Chrysalis

An Ant running around in the sunshine looking for food came across a Chrysalis nearing its time of change. The Chrysalis moved its tail, and the Ant noticed for the first time that the creature was alive. "You poor suffering thing!" cried the Ant. "How unfortunate that I can run here and there as fast as I like—even climb the tallest trees—while you hang imprisoned here in that shell with only the power to move your scaly tail!" The Chrysalis heard this, but did not reply. A few days later, when the Ant passed that way again, nothing but the shell remained. The Ant wondered what had become of the creature inside. Suddenly he felt himself shaded and fanned by the gorgeous wings of a beautiful butterfly. "Hello, Ant," said the Butterfly. "Remember me? Your sad, pitiable friend? Brag now of your powers to run and climb—as long as you can get me to listen!" At that, the Butterfly rose into the air and floated away on a summer breeze, never again to be seen by the Ant.

Do not be deceived by appearances.

CAST OF CHARACTERS

CHRYS, female, pretty, smart, talented, paralyzed from the waist down.

ANDY, male, same age, plays basketball, but lacks game.

(CHRYS, a pretty girl, sits in a wheelchair, drawing. ANDY enters miming playing basketball. He stops and dribbles the ball, trying to look impressive.)

ANDY: Hey there.

CHRYS: Hello.

ANDY: Whatcha drawing?

CHRYS: Just...drawing.

ANDY: O-kaay... Can I see it?

CHRYS: I'm not done yet.

ANDY: I'm Andy. Moved here a few weeks ago. *(Beat.)* What's your name?

CHRYS: Chrys.

ANDY: Saw you hanging out on the sidelines today. Seen you there before. You were drawing then too.

CHRYS: Yep!

ANDY: *(Beat.)* Just finished practice. Waiting for my mom. *(Beat.)* You might have noticed me on the team. Did you see my offense today? Might be shooting guard before the year is out.

CHRYS: Who knows!

ANDY: You come to all the games?

CHRYS: I like sports.

ANDY: The team at my old school was pretty good. Nationally ranked.

CHRYS: That's cool.

ANDY: *(Shrugs nonchalantly:)* I played point guard. Pretty much in charge.

(He takes a shot and misses.)

Whoah! I missed. Guess I'm tired after practice today.

(He dribbles the ball.)

I just need to train harder. That's the problem with most people. They don't take stuff seriously. Someday I plan to go pro.

(He dribbles, and goes through an elaborate, somewhat silly "focus" routine, to get ready to shoot. He sneaks glances at her. She is concentrating on her drawing. Finally he shoots. And misses. He runs to get the ball.)

Geez! I probably need some potassium or something.

(He puts the ball down and stretches.)

Wow... I guess it was rude of me to go on about playing—when you, when you're...

CHRYS: When I'm...?

ANDY: Never mind. *(Beat.)* Come on, what are you drawing? Can I see?

(He moves to look at the drawing. She turns her pad over so he can't see it. After a while he goes back to stretching.)

Do you wish you could play ball?

CHRYS: I do.

ANDY: I'm sorry. That's too bad.

CHRYS: That I play ball?

ANDY: What? No, I meant... Wait. You play?

CHRYS: Believe it or not.

ANDY: No offense, but are you pulling my leg? *(Beat.)* Oh wow—oops. I didn't mean... To bring up, uh...

CHRYS: What... Legs?

ANDY: Right.

CHRYS: Um... It's OK to talk about legs in my presence. *(Beat.)* If you want to ask a question about mine, just ask.

ANDY: What? No... I don't—

CHRYS: Yes you do. I can tell. I get that look a lot. *(Beat.)* Ask, then.

ANDY: OK. *(He takes a deep breath:)* Where do you play?

CHRYS: Local league.

ANDY: But—how do you play?

CHRYS: *(Focused expression:)* Like this.

(Chrys makes a goofy face and mimes dribbling the ball.)

Sorry. I couldn't help myself. *(She laughs:)* Should see the look on your face. *(Beat.)* It's a fair question. There's rules about our chairs and stuff—like what kinds we can use, but otherwise it's pretty much the same as what you play.

ANDY: Oh. Good for you, for—playing.

(Andy goes back to dribbling. Chrys goes back to drawing. While she is concentrating, he sneaks over to look at her drawing.)

Wow...

(She quickly turns her sketch-pad over.)

CHRYS: I'm not done yet!

ANDY: Is one of those people me?

CHRYS: Yes.

ANDY: *(Beat.)* It's really good. Can I see more?

(After a moment she begins to flip through the pad.)

Wow! You drew everybody on the team! It looks like us too—your drawings are so real... We really look like we're moving! Even the muscles in our arms—how do you do that?!

(She laughs.)

CHRYS: I just—pay attention, I guess.

ANDY: Cool. It's really cool that you can draw like that.

(Andy takes another shot and misses. He runs to get the ball.)

Geez! Missed again! Guess I'm a little...nervous.

CHRYS: Nervous? About what?

ANDY: I...I wanted to ask you a question.

CHRYS: Ask away!

ANDY: You know I'm new here and everything, and I've, well, I've been noticing you. It seems like you...really know your way around.

CHRYS: *(Smiles at his awkwardness:)* I've been with the same class since kindergarten.

ANDY: What I mean is, I wondered if maybe...you'd like to show me around the neighborhood—after school sometime? We could get ice cream or something. I could push your chair for you!

CHRYS: *(Laughs a little:)* That's OK, Andy. I can get around pretty well myself.

ANDY: Oh. Cool. That's cool...so...?

CHRYS: Sure, Andy. I'll show you around sometime.

ANDY: Awesome!

(He misses his shot again.)

Ahhh! Man... O for O! *(Beat.)* I'm really glad you said yes. I mean, I was pretty sure you would, but I was still sweating it some.

CHRYS: *(Beat.)* What made you so sure I would say yes?

ANDY: Well, you're super pretty, but with your legs...well, I bet you don't have a boyfriend or anything. I mean, probably not everybody sees past your — chair.

CHRYS: Excuse me?

ANDY: Which is too bad for them, because obviously you are pretty and talented.

CHRYS: Uh...

ANDY: I mean, those pictures you draw! It's really cool you can draw like that. Especially since watching everybody out there must make you kind of sad.

CHRYS: What?

ANDY: It must be really hard for you to sit here and watch everybody running and stuff.

CHRYS: What do you mean?

(He dribbles the ball as he talks.)

ANDY: I mean — watching everybody using their legs! Just imagine how much better you could play if you could run and stuff! *(Beat.)* That's why you do these drawings! So you can imagine what it would be like to move around like regular people, right? *(Long beat.)* Chrys? Hello? *(Beat.)* Did I say something wrong?

(Chrys moves over to him and knocks the mimed ball out of his hands. She dribbles it, picks it up, and makes the shot.)

Wow... That was... How did you make that shot?

CHRYS: Andy, I think I'll let you show yourself around.

(She begins to exit, but turns back.)

By the way, the reason I draw is because it helps to know how the body moves, since someday I plan to be a sports medicine doctor. Maybe I'll be so good I'll be able to fix your game. Good luck to you.

(She exits. End of play.)

CHEER SQUAD
by Jeff Goode

after Aesop's fable *The Two Crabs*

A Crab and its Mother were walking along the beach. "Child," said the Mother, "you should try to walk straighter, instead of scuttling along sideways."

"Pray, mother," said the young Crab, "do but set the example and I will gladly follow you."

It is better to lead by example.

CAST OF CHARACTERS

ANNE, bossy cheerleader.

TRACY, novice cheerleader.

DIANA, gossipy cheerleader.

(Lights up on ANNE and TRACY, two cheerleaders, practicing. Their school crest is a cheerful crab.)

ANNE & TRACY: Gimme an A! Gimme an E! Gimme an S-O-P! Put 'em all together and what's that spell? AESOP! AESOP!! YAAAAY!!!!

(They jump up and down. Tracy is very peppy. Anne abruptly stops practicing.)

ANNE: Okay, that's great. But keep your arms straight on the poms, and on the turn, lead with your right foot not the left.

TRACY: But you led with your left.

ANNE: Okay, look. You're new here so I'm going to pretend you didn't just try to tell me how to do a routine I've been doing since you were, like, a freshman. I know what I did. I don't need you to tell me. There's different ways of doing things. We don't all have to be the same.

TRACY: But I thought you said—

ANNE: It's okay, I'm not mad. It's just, it's not cool to correct other people on their routine. It makes you look like a know-it-all diva. And not in a good way.

TRACY: But I didn't—

ANNE: And it's pronounced "Eeesop." Not "Aaysop."

TRACY: Oh, I thought it was "Aaysop."

ANNE: That doesn't even sound right.

TRACY: I thought both were correct.

ANNE: No, it's "Eesop."

TRACY: Because Mr. Doukas says "Aaysop."

(Silence. Anne just glares.)

And he's the history teacher.

(*Silence. Anne just glares.*)

And he's Greek.

ANNE: Okay, look, it doesn't matter how it's pronounced, because there are different ways to pronounce it and it's not polite to make fun of the way other people say things. If you're gonna act like a diva, maybe you just shouldn't be on cheer squad.

TRACY: Sorry.

ANNE: It's okay, you'll catch on. Just follow my lead and do what I do and you'll be perfect. Okay?

TRACY: Okay...

ANNE: (*Suddenly shouting offstage:*) Jennifer, no!! You're doing it all wrong!! Do it like I told you!

(*Anne rushes out. DIANA, who has been lurking, suddenly comes over.*)

DIANA: What was that all about?

TRACY: (*Startled:*) Huh? Oh, hi.

DIANA: What did you say to set her off like that?

TRACY: Nothing.

DIANA: Oh, come on. I saw you talking to her. Is it a secret? You can tell me.

TRACY: It was nothing.

DIANA: Was it really nothing? Or did she tell you to tell me it was nothing, but really it's something?

TRACY: It was really nothing.

DIANA: Aha! I knew it! Okay, look, I know you're new here. But this is cheer squad. We're a team. We're like sisters.

TRACY: Right.

DIANA: Only we're nice to each other.

TRACY: Okay.

DIANA: So we don't keep secrets. And we don't gossip. If she said something about me behind my back and made you promise not to tell anyone, then you have to tell me.

TRACY: It wasn't anything. Honest. She was just correcting me on my cheers.

DIANA: Oh my G! She really did that? You must think she's a total diva.

TRACY: No, I don't.

DIANA: It's okay, if you do. That's what everybody says about her.

TRACY: They do?

DIANA: Everybody. You know what else they say?

TRACY: What? What do they say?

DIANA: Wouldn't you like to know? You are so nosy. I bet if I tell you, it'll be all over cheer squad by tomorrow.

TRACY: No, it won't.

DIANA: You'll keep it a secret?

TRACY: Yes, I promise!

DIANA: Aha! So you <u>will</u> keep it a secret.

TRACY: I mean, no, I won't keep it a secret, but I won't tell anyone either—!

DIANA: Aha!

TRACY: Ooh, I don't know what's the right answer.

DIANA: Look, it's okay, I'm not mad. It's just, it's not cool to keep secrets from the rest of the squad and talk about them behind their back. It makes you look like you're not a team player.

TRACY: I'm a team player.

DIANA: Like you're a backstabber.

TRACY: I'm not a backstabber.

DIANA: All right, I don't believe you, but I'm gonna let it slide this time, since it's your first day. But from now on, no secrets.

TRACY: No secrets.

DIANA: And no gossip.

TRACY: You got it.

DIANA: Like sisters.

TRACY: Like sisters.

DIANA: Who like each other.

TRACY: Right.

DIANA: We're a team. So there's no alliances.

TRACY: But isn't that what a team is? An alliance?

DIANA: There's no secret alliances!!

TRACY: Okay.

DIANA: Look, just follow my lead and you'll be fine.

TRACY: Gotcha.

DIANA: Uh oh, here she comes. We never had this conversation.

TRACY: But you said...

(*Anne enters.*)

ANNE: What's going on here? What are you two talking about?

DIANA: Nothing.

ANNE: (*Threatening:*) Tracy?

TRACY: Nothing!

ANNE: Did she tell you not to tell me what you were talking about?

TRACY: No! I mean, yes! I mean, sort of.

DIANA: Why would you say that?!

TRACY: Because it's true!

ANNE: Then why don't I believe you?

(*She glowers suspiciously.*)

DIANA: (*Suddenly blurts:*) You think you know everything, but you don't!!

ANNE: How would you know?

DIANA: Tracy told me.

ANNE: What?!

TRACY: No, I didn't.

ANNE: Liar!

DIANA: Wow, you really are a liar. We just talked about it.

ANNE: You were talking about me behind my back?

TRACY: Not on purpose.

DIANA: *(Shaking her head:)* Such a liar.

ANNE: We have a zero tolerance for gossip in cheer squad.

DIANA: And lying.

ANNE: And lying!

DIANA: And bossing people around.

ANNE: She's bossy, too?

DIANA: She seems like the type.

TRACY: What?!

ANNE: Look, Tracy, cheer squad is about trust. When you're doing a front flip off a human pyramid into a cradle catch, you've got to know that the other cheer-members have got your back.

DIANA: Or your front, if it's a back flip.

ANNE: If we can't count on you not to be a backstabbing…

DIANA: Gossipy…

ANNE: Know-it-all…

DIANA: Diva snitch…

ANNE: Well, then I don't know why we let you on the team in the first place.

DIANA: Except that the school makes us. We have to take everybody.

ANNE: We're not mad.

DIANA: We're really not.

ANNE: But you just have to stop trying to do everything your way, and follow our lead until you get the hang of it. Okay? Is that so hard?

TRACY: No, I guess, I understand. I wouldn't want to be all those terrible things you just accused me of. But if you give me a second chance, I promise I'll always try to follow your example.

ANNE & DIANA: Good.

TRACY: That is... Assuming you know how to set one. *(Suddenly shouting offstage:)* Jennifer! No! That's not how it's done! *(Exiting:)* Later, Divas.

(Tracy walks out. Anne and Diana are flabbergasted.)

ANNE: *(Pause.)* Did she just call us...?

DIANA: I like her.

(End of play.)

THE RAVEN AND THE SWAN
by Dave Ulrich

after Aesop's fable *The Raven and the Swan*

A Raven saw a Swan swimming in the lake and wished to have the same beautiful plumage. Believing the Swan's look came from the waters in which it swam, the Raven left home to cleanse its feathers day and night, but failed to change their color.

A change of habit cannot change nature.

CAST OF CHARACTERS

A GREEN-HAIRED KID
A PURPLE-HAIRED KID

(Note: Although this was written for two males, it could work with two females instead. However, I would not recommend one of each, as it will introduce an unintended dynamic. Also, the script uses lighting cues to indicate the passage of time, but performance space limitations may require directors to find more inventive methods of illustrating nightfall and sunrise.)

(A GREEN-HAIRED KID enters. He is tapping a soccer ball on his toe, trying to keep it in the air for as long as he can. He passes a PURPLE-HAIRED KID who is sitting on the curb. The Green-Haired Kid notices the other kid and loses his concentration, making the ball roll away.)

GREEN-HAIRED KID: What's wrong with your hair?

PURPLE-HAIRED KID: Who? Me?

GREEN-HAIRED KID: Of course you. Your hair is violet.

PURPLE-HAIRED KID: It's purple. Duh.

GREEN-HAIRED KID: I've never seen purple hair.

PURPLE-HAIRED KID: You should get out more.

GREEN-HAIRED KID: Is that what you do?

PURPLE-HAIRED KID: What are you talking about?

GREEN-HAIRED KID: Do you go outside a lot?

PURPLE-HAIRED KID: Yeah, I guess.

GREEN-HAIRED KID: That must be why your hair's funny.

PURPLE-HAIRED KID: My hair's not funny.

GREEN-HAIRED KID: Then why isn't it like mine?

PURPLE-HAIRED KID: Don't know. Guess I'm just special.

GREEN-HAIRED KID: No, I'm the special one.

PURPLE-HAIRED KID: Then why aren't you purple like me?

GREEN-HAIRED KID: Maybe I will be.

PURPLE-HAIRED KID: How?

GREEN-HAIRED KID: I'll do what you do. I'll go outside a lot, too. So much that my hair will be even purpler than yours.

PURPLE-HAIRED KID: That's stupid.

GREEN-HAIRED KID: You're stupid. And you'll feel stupid when you see how purple I'll be.

(The Green-Haired Kid sits next to the Purple-Haired Kid in the same way, and same position.)

PURPLE-HAIRED KID: Why are you doing what I do?

GREEN-HAIRED KID: I'm making my hair purple.

PURPLE-HAIRED KID: You're deranged.

GREEN-HAIRED KID: You're just jealous because my hair's gonna be like yours.

PURPLE-HAIRED KID: I'm not jealous. I'm worried.

GREEN-HAIRED KID: About what?

PURPLE-HAIRED KID: About having a crazy person sitting so close to me.

GREEN-HAIRED KID: Then go inside and turn your hair green.

PURPLE-HAIRED KID: I was here first.

GREEN-HAIRED KID: Stay, go, I don't care. I'll be right here.

PURPLE-HAIRED KID: But this is my spot. *(Pointing:)* And that is my house. So how long do you plan on ruining my day?

GREEN-HAIRED KID: I'm only gonna be here until my hair is more purple than yours.

PURPLE-HAIRED KID: Whatever.

(The Purple-Haired Kid stands up.)

GREEN-HAIRED KID: See, you're already jealous of my purple hair.

PURPLE-HAIRED KID: Sitting here won't change your hair. It doesn't work that way!

GREEN-HAIRED KID: Sure it won't. Jealous much?

PURPLE-HAIRED KID: You don't have purple hair!

GREEN-HAIRED KID: Yet.

(The Purple-Haired Kid stomps off. The Green-Haired Kid hugs his knees and absorbs the sun's rays. The lights go down and he stretches out. The lights go back up and he sits up again. The Purple-Haired Kid returns.)

PURPLE-HAIRED KID: You're still here.

GREEN-HAIRED KID: Is my hair more purple than yours?

PURPLE-HAIRED KID: No.

GREEN-HAIRED KID: Then I'll be here awhile longer.

PURPLE-HAIRED KID: Your hair is exactly the same shade as before.

GREEN-HAIRED KID: I doubt that.

PURPLE-HAIRED KID: Whatever.

(The Purple-Haired Kid walks off. The soccer ball rolls back in toward the Green-Haired Kid who catches it.)

GREEN-HAIRED KID: *(Shouting off toward the exit:)* You can't trick me! I won't be distracted! *(To himself:)* I'm not giving up.

PURPLE-HAIRED KID: *(From offstage:)* You're welcome.

(The Green-Haired Kid rolls the ball around in his hands. He bounces it a little, then lays back and leans his head on it – like a pillow. But then it slips out and his head falls. Finally, he hugs it and curls up with it in his arms as he goes to sleep, while the lights go down again. When the lights come up, the Green-Haired Kid is lying flat on his back motionless. The soccer ball a few feet away. The Purple-Haired Kid enters with a plate of food and a bottle of water.)

Hello? *(Beat.)* Hell-ooooo.

(The Purple-Haired Kid places the food and water next to the Green-Haired kid and picks up the soccer ball. He bounces it once.)

Hey. I brought you some food and water...even though you're very annoying.

(He kicks the soccer ball for a short beat and stops.)

Kid, you need to eat and drink. It's been like two whole days.

(Pause as he looks for a reaction, but the Green-Haired Kid doesn't move.)

Wake up.

(Still no movement. The Purple-Haired Kid steps closer.)

Hey, your hair's purple now.

(The Green-Haired Kid sits up so fast it startles the Purple-Haired Kid who jumps backward.)

GREEN-HAIRED KID: Really?

PURPLE-HAIRED KID: Totally.

GREEN-HAIRED KID: Cool! *(Seeing the food:)* Is that for me?

PURPLE-HAIRED KID: Yeah, but I need the plate back or my Mom will kill me.

(The Green-Haired Kid tears into the food ravenously.)

GREEN-HAIRED KID: *(As he eats:)* Are you being nice because I have purple hair now, too?

PURPLE-HAIRED KID: No. I actually preferred you with green hair. I was really jealous.

GREEN-HAIRED KID: *(Slows his eating:)* You were?

PURPLE-HAIRED KID: Yeah, you should go back.

GREEN-HAIRED KID: How?

PURPLE-HAIRED KID: Well, how'd you change it?

GREEN-HAIRED KID: Stayed outside a lot.

PURPLE-HAIRED KID: So go home and stay in. I bet it'll change right back.

GREEN-HAIRED KID: Really?

PURPLE-HAIRED KID: Yeah. And when you're you again...maybe you should...come by sometime.

(The Purple-Haired Kid goes offstage kicking the soccer ball.)

GREEN-HAIRED KID: *(Shouting off:)* I will! I'll have green hair in no time. The greenest! You'll see!

PURPLE-HAIRED KID: *(From offstage:)* Whatever.

(The lights go down on the Green-Haired Kid. End of play.)

THE STUDENT AND THE MATHEMATICIAN
by Adam Hahn

after Aesop's fable *Hercules and the Wagoner*

A wagoner was driving a heavy load on a muddy path. The wheels began to sink in the mud, and the horses pulled until the wagon was stuck. The wagoner knelt by the path and prayed to Hercules the Strong for help. Hercules appeared to him and said, "Get up, put your shoulder to the wheel, and push!"

Self help is the best help.

CAST OF CHARACTERS

DAVID, a male student.

ONE, male, plays Father, Professor Eeeunf, narrates.

TWO, female, plays Mrs. Heffesfeffen, Aunt Jane, narrates.

(DAVID sits at a desk. TWO stands, ready to teach as "Mrs. Heffesfeffen." ONE narrates.)

TWO: Good morning class!

ONE: Mrs. Heffesfeffen was a math teacher.

DAVID: Good morning, Mrs. Heffesfeffen.

ONE: David was a student.

TWO: I hope that the whispering I hear in the back of the room will come to an end soon, unlike the digits of pi! HA HA HA! That was a math joke!

ONE: Mrs. Heffesfeffen was an enthusiastic math teacher.

DAVID: Mrs. Heffesfeffen, this is boring.

ONE: Not all of Mrs. Heffesfeffen's students appreciated her enthusiasm.

DAVID: This is possibly the most boring thing I have ever experienced.

ONE: David did not appreciate it at all.

DAVID: Given the choice between studying math and watching paint dry, I would rather watch paint dry.

ONE: David was vocal about his lack of appreciation.

DAVID: Even if it was special paint that dried really slowly, you know, special slow-drying, extra-boring paint?

ONE: David was a little too vocal, if you ask me.

DAVID: Even if it wasn't actual paint drying, but just a video of paint drying, and even if I'd already seen that video a dozen times—

ONE: David was a rude, lazy, ungrateful—

TWO: It's all right! Not all students see the beauty in mathematics right away.

ONE: Mrs. Heffesfeffen tried to make the best of the situation.

TWO: David, why do you think math is boring?

DAVID: Because I'm never going to use math in real life!

TWO: No?

DAVID: No! And if I ever need to, a calculator will do all the work, right?

TWO: Well, David, when the Giant Yellow Butterfly People from Ganymede take over the earth, the first thing they'll do is break open all the calculators and eat the batteries, because tiny batteries are like candy to the Giant Yellow Butterfly People. The only way to send them back to the moons of Jupiter will be to overload the communications system on their mothership with a precisely timed satellite broadcast. It's going to take a lot of math to coordinate that broadcast, and you won't have a calculator to help you, and if you fail all of mankind will be slaves to the Giant Yellow Butterfly People forever. Is that really what you want, David?

ONE: It's possible that Mrs. Heffesfeffen was barking mad.

TWO: No I'm not! I'm kidding! That was a math joke.

ONE: No, it really wasn't.

TWO: HA HA HA HA HA HA HA HA HA HA HA HA HA HA!

DAVID: Can I just get the homework assignment and leave?

TWO: Yes, and you'll be happy to know that your homework this weekend is just one problem.

DAVID: I hope it's not another story problem set on a farm.

TWO: On Joe's farm, there are forty acres of cornfields and sixty acres of soybean fields.

DAVID: If farmers do math all the time, I am definitely not going to be a farmer.

TWO: One acre produces one hundred sixty bushels of corn or forty-five bushels of soybeans. Corn sells for six dollars per bushel, and soybeans sell for ten dollars per bushel. Joe loses one-fourth of his corn and one-fifth of his soybeans in an unfortunate silo-fire. What fraction of his total revenue comes from the sale of soybeans?

DAVID: How am I supposed to figure that out?

TWO: You can do it. Just multiply, multiply again, multiply by a fraction, three more multiplications for the beans, add, divide, and simplify the fraction you end up with by finding the greatest common factor.

DAVID: How am I supposed to stay awake while working on this boring problem?

TWO: Remember the Giant Yellow Butterfly People are on their way! HA HA HA HA HA HA!

ONE: I don't think she's kidding.

(One exits, Two takes over narration:)

TWO: So David went home, where he briefly considered sitting down and doing his homework —

DAVID: Boring! This would take forever —

TWO: Probably under fifteen minutes —

DAVID: Maybe I can ask someone for help.

(Enter One, as "Father.")

TWO: David found his father.

DAVID: Dad, can you believe I have to go to math class every day? Can you imagine sitting in a chair and listening to someone talk about something completely boring for FIFTY MINUTES?!

ONE: Son, I have a job. Sometimes I listen to people talk about boring things all day.

TWO: That's actually a big part of what it means to have a job.

DAVID: I didn't open this father-son dialogue to listen to your problems. Are you going to help me with my homework or not?

ONE: Help you? You just need to multiply, multiply again, multiply by a fraction, do three more multiplications for the beans—

DAVID: Whoa, Dad, I don't want this problem to take all day—

TWO: Probably under fifteen minutes.

ONE: Well, I don't see another way to do this. You could ask your Aunt Jane—

DAVID: That's right, Aunt Jane, the engineer! She does math every day!

(Exit Two. One narrates:)

ONE: And David went in search of his Aunt Jane, because engineers are people who enjoy using math and science to solve problems.

(Enter Two as "Aunt Jane":)

TWO: I have a job developing scratch-resistant plastics!

ONE: Some of them enjoy it too much.

DAVID: Hi, Aunt Jane.

TWO: David, your father told me you might be coming. Would you like a tour of my lab?

DAVID: No thanks.

TWO: We've been working on a new toilet seat that's impossible to scratch. Would you like to try to scratch it?

DAVID: No.

TWO: Are you sure?

DAVID: Yes.

TWO: Are you really sure you don't want to scratch my toilet seat?

ONE: This part of the conversation went on longer than it needed to.

TWO: You can try with your fingernails—

DAVID: No—

TWO: Or sandpaper—

DAVID: No—

TWO: Or a grinding wheel—

DAVID: Jane, I really just want help with a math problem.

TWO: Your father told me! The one where you need to multiply, multiply again, multiply by a fraction—

DAVID: Jane, I came here because I thought you could help me find the answer without all the multiplication—

TWO: You want to solve Farmer Joe's corn and soybean revenue problem without all the multiplication?! What fun would that be?

ONE: David tried to put this into terms that an engineer would understand.

DAVID: As much fun as the multiplication is, I thought it could be more fun if there was a way to get to the answer in fewer steps.

TWO: Ooooooooh. So you're going for efficiency.

DAVID: Yes?

TWO: Awesome.

DAVID: Can you help me?

(Exit One.)

TWO: David, I know who you need to talk to.

DAVID: Who?

TWO: Professor Eeeunf.

DAVID: Professor Eeeunf?

(Two narrates:)

TWO: In the mathematics department of a nearby university worked the world-famous Professor Julius Johannes Josiah Jeremiah Steven Eeeunf. David went to see him.

(Enter One as "Professor Eeeunf.")

DAVID: Professor Eeeunf?

ONE: My boy, call me Steve. All of my mathematician friends call me Steve.

DAVID: Steve, is it true that you know a lot about math?

TWO: This is a bit like asking a dog if he knows a lot about being hairy and smelling bad.

ONE: I teach courses on functional analysis, vector calculus, linear systems, nonlinear differential equations, ring theory, set theory, probability, and stochastic processes. My boy, I know a lot about math.

TWO: A little impressed, but already starting to get bored, David showed Professor Eeeunf his homework.

DAVID: On Joe's farm—

ONE: I know all about Joe's farm! I wrote my doctoral dissertation on the limits of Cartesian geometry as applied to Joe's farm!

DAVID: Can you help me?

ONE: I can! Pencil ready? Now multiply!

TWO: David multiplied.

ONE: And again!

TWO: David multiplied again.

ONE: Now multiply by a fraction!

DAVID: Wait a second—

ONE: Keep going! Multiply three more times for the beans!

TWO: Under Professor Eeeunf's direction, David did the work he could have done when he first got home from school.

DAVID: So boring!

ONE: This is the best part! You're going to find the greatest common factor!

DAVID: We've been doing this forever!

TWO: After about fifteen minutes, he was done.

ONE: Congratulations, my boy. You have done your homework!

TWO: And he was learning math whether he had enjoyed it or not.

DAVID: I didn't enjoy it.

TWO: And years later, when the Giant Yellow Butterfly People invaded the earth, David was ready for them.

DAVID: Wait, what?

(End of play.)

CAN'T FORGET
by Liz Shannon Miller

after Aesop's fable The Laborer and the Snake

A poisonous snake bit the infant son of a farmer, killing him, and the farmer decided to kill the snake in retaliation. He swung his axe too hastily, though, and only chopped off the snake's tail. Afraid that the snake would bite him as revenge for the loss of his tail, the farmer tried to make things up to the snake with a gift of bread and salt, but the snake was not interested. "We can never be friends, because I will always remind you of the loss of your son, and you will always remind me of the loss of my tail."

No matter how much you apologize, some wounds will never heal.

CAST OF CHARACTERS

FOX, a teenage girl fox.
MOUSE, a girl mouse around the same age.

(Night. The front porch of a house. FOX, a teenage girl fox, carries a box of stuff up to the front door of the house, depositing it on the house's welcome mat. She looks at it for a moment, then, changing her mind about something, retrieves a photo from the box, tucking it into her back pocket. Then, almost urgently, she turns away from the door to leave — MOUSE, a girl mouse around the same age, opens the front door. Her voice catches Fox by surprise.)

MOUSE: Sneaking away so soon?

FOX: *(Uncomfortable:)* Hi, Mouse.

MOUSE: Oh, cool, you do remember my name. I wasn't sure.

FOX: Look, I just wanted to get you your stuff back—

MOUSE: You mean the stuff I'd left at my former best friend's house? Awesome. Thanks. I appreciate it. I really didn't trust her to hold onto it anymore.

FOX: Well, now you have it back. Enjoy.

(Fox moves to exit again. Mouse looks in the box.)

MOUSE: I don't see my sweater.

FOX: You said I could keep it.

MOUSE: No, I said that it looked better on you than me. But I guess can understand how you'd be confused. About whose sweater it was. You don't really seem to care about other people's stuff, after all.

FOX: Oh, stop it!

MOUSE: Why should I?

FOX: Because I am trying to apologize to you, okay?

MOUSE: *(Fake confused:)* Really? Apologize for what?

FOX: For... Okay, I'm not totally sure.

MOUSE: Think about it. Think about it really really hard.

FOX: I know you don't like that I've started dating Badger—

MOUSE: And why could that be?

FOX: I seriously do not know. All I know is that you've got half the forest calling me names behind my back—

MOUSE: You can't prove I started any of that—

FOX: Even if I can't, a real friend would be defending me! And I saw you talking with those bluejays just the other day and you know I saw you shut up when I got close.

MOUSE: It was a private conversation.

FOX: About me, right?

MOUSE: Look, I don't even see why you care. I bet Badger's expecting you right now.

FOX: He can wait.

MOUSE: I don't even get why you're going out with him. I mean, he's not that popular.

FOX: He's nice. And smart. We have fun together.

MOUSE: Hanging out in his badger hole?

FOX: Sometimes. Yeah. What's it to you?

MOUSE: Nothing. Absolutely nothing. Have a nice night.

(She moves to close the door.)

FOX: Oh my god. You're jealous.

(Mouse hesitates.)

MOUSE: No, I'm not.

FOX: You totally are. Why are you jealous of me and Badger?

MOUSE: Um, who said?

FOX: Mouse, you and I have been sworn BFFs since forever—

MOUSE: —don't say BFF. That's what my mom says when she's trying to sound cool—

FOX: —I totally know what you're thinking, okay?

MOUSE: Really? Because if we're best friends, if you know everything about me, then how come you had no idea that I've liked Badger for years?

FOX: *(Stunned:)* Um. Because you didn't tell me?

MOUSE: Right.

FOX: No, seriously! You've liked Badger this whole time?

MOUSE: I know, it's stupid.

FOX: It's not! Why didn't you tell me?

MOUSE: Because it was stupid!

FOX: It's not stupid to like somebody!

MOUSE: It is if you're me and your best friend is you, all lanky and fast and gorgeous... It makes sense for Badger to notice you. It made no sense for Badger to notice me.

FOX: But you're great! You're smart and cute and nice—

MOUSE: You really think so?

FOX: Well, I did until you started telling everyone all that stuff about me.

MOUSE: Right. Yeah.

FOX: Look, I'm really sorry about Badger. I had no idea. And if I had known—

MOUSE: You'd have done exactly the same thing?

FOX: Yes! Maybe. No. I don't know.

MOUSE: But you're not going to break up with him now, are you?

FOX: He's the only one saying nice things about me at the moment, so yeah. Probably not.

MOUSE: Okay.

FOX: I should probably get going. I'm... Look, I'm not sorry about me and Badger. But I am sorry that we couldn't talk about it.

MOUSE: Thanks. I guess. And I'm sorry about all those rumors.

FOX: The ones you didn't start?

MOUSE: Yeah.

FOX: Okay. I'll see you later.

(She starts to exit. Mouse picks up the box, looking through it again.)

MOUSE: Hey, Fox?

FOX: What?

MOUSE: I — Is that photo of us in here?

FOX: What photo?

MOUSE: Oh, the one from when we were really little, at the lake?

FOX: When we both fell in —

MOUSE: — and got covered in mud —

FOX: —and had to spend the rest of the day getting bathed by our moms?

MOUSE: Yeah.

(They smile at the shared memory. For just a moment.)

FOX: Um. I don't know. I'll have to check at home. Do you want it if I can find it?

MOUSE: Oh, no. No. You can keep it. I don't care about it, really. I was just curious.

FOX: Okay. Well. If I find it, maybe I can make you a copy.

MOUSE: I don't really care that much.

FOX: Right.

MOUSE: Okay.

FOX: I'll see you later, Mouse.

MOUSE: Yeah. Later, Fox.

(She grabs the box and closes the door, exiting. A long beat. Fox pulls the photo out of her pocket. Looking at it for a moment.)

FOX: Best friends forever.

(End of play.)

THE LION AND THE BOAR
by Mike Rothschild

after Aesop's fable *The Lion and the Boar*

One scorching summer day, a Lion and a Boar found a small well at the same time. Since they were both equally thirsty, they argued over who should drink first. Their argument turned into a fight, and they attacked each other without mercy. After stopping to catch their breath before fighting again, they noticed a pack of Vultures hovering above them, waiting for one of them to win so they could feast on the loser. Seeing the Vultures circling, they immediately agreed to share the water.

It is better to be friends than become the food of Crows or Vultures.

CAST OF CHARACTERS

LOUIE, a boy.
BOBBY, a boy.
VIC THE BULLY, a bully.

(*Lights up on two kids, LOUIE and BOBBY. There is a table in the middle, with a package of cupcakes. There's one left.*)

LOUIE: Can you believe the gym teacher? He made us run so much.

BOBBY: I know! We weren't even running anywhere. Just running.

LOUIE: So much running.

(*They stumble on the cupcake.*)

Oh, there's a cupcake left.

BOBBY: I thought they were all gone.

LOUIE: I guess they aren't. You want it, Bobby?

BOBBY: No, you take it, Louie.

LOUIE: Are you sure? I don't want to take it if you want it.

BOBBY: You can have it.

LOUIE: I shouldn't. My mom will yell at me for spoiling my dinner.

BOBBY: Why do they always say that? It's not like I can't eat a cupcake AND dinner AND another cupcake.

LOUIE: Or a pie.

BOBBY: A pie?

LOUIE: What? I'm a hearty eater.

BOBBY: Fine. You can have the cupcake.

LOUIE: No, seriously, you take it.

BOBBY: You really don't want it?

LOUIE: No!

BOBBY: I don't want it either.

(They look at each other.)

Okay, I'll take it.

(He reaches for it. Louie pouts.)

LOUIE: Oh.

BOBBY: You said you didn't want it.

LOUIE: So did you!

BOBBY: I don't!

LOUIE: Then why are you taking it?

BOBBY: Because you said you didn't want it. I don't want it to go to waste. Just because I'm taking it doesn't mean I want it.

(He reaches for it again.)

LOUIE: I mean, yeah, I WANT it...

BOBBY: ...me too.

LOUIE: Even though you said you didn't want it.

BOBBY: I do want it.

LOUIE: So do I! Let's just play rock paper scissors.

BOBBY: Okay, that's fair.

(They play rock paper scissors. Louie is a rock, Bobby is paper.)

Winner!

LOUIE: That's not fair! Let's split it!

BOBBY: I just won!

LOUIE: Two out of three!

BOBBY: But I won! AND you said I could have it!

LOUIE: And you said *I* could have it!

BOBBY: I did, didn't I? Why don't we just split it? That way, we each get some, but neither of us spoil our dinner.

LOUIE: That's totally fair. I'll just take the top half.

BOBBY: That's the part with the frosting. The frosting is the best part! Who wants just the cake part of a cupcake?

LOUIE: I thought you might.

BOBBY: I don't. We'll split it down the middle. Do you have a knife?

LOUIE: I'm not allowed to touch anything sharp.

BOBBY: I can see that. I'll just rip it in half.

LOUIE: No, I will!

BOBBY: What, you don't trust me?

LOUIE: Of course I do.

BOBBY: Then left me rip it in half.

LOUIE: I don't trust you.

BOBBY: I don't trust YOU!

(Bobby reaches for the cupcake.)

LOUIE: You're doing it wrong!

(Louie makes a grab for the cupcake, while Bobby tries to hold him off. Just then, VIC THE BULLY walks on, staring down both of them.)

VIC THE BULLY: Nice cupcake you got there.

(Bobby and Louie stop fighting.)

LOUIE: Oh boy.

VIC THE BULLY: Yeah. Oh boy.

BOBBY: What do you want, Vic?

VIC THE BULLY: I want that cupcake. And you're going to give it to me.

BOBBY: Why? It's our cupcake.

VIC THE BULLY: Not anymore. It's mine. And you can't do anything about it.

(Vic starts to walk toward them.)

BOBBY: Wait, give us a second!

VIC THE BULLY: Sure. I can beat you up whenever I want.

(Bobby and Louie huddle.)

BOBBY: *(To Louie:)* He's not going to beat us up over a cupcake.

LOUIE: Yeah he will! They don't call him Vic the Bully because he's a really misunderstood nice guy!

VIC THE BULLY: No, I'm really quite misunderstood. And I'm totally going to beat you up over a cupcake.

(He continues to slowly walk toward them.)

LOUIE: You said you'd wait!

VIC THE BULLY: I did. Three whole seconds.

BOBBY: Okay, you distract him, I'll run away with the cupcake.

LOUIE: What? No, you distract him and I'll run away. I'm on the track team.

BOBBY: You also eat an entire pie in one sitting!

VIC THE BULLY: That's disgusting.

(Vic is now right on top of them, and the boys start to back off.)

BOBBY: We have to do something! If we can't make up our minds, he's just going to take it from us.

LOUIE: You're right.

VIC THE BULLY: He's right.

LOUIE: So let's work together.

(He rips the cupcake in half and gives half to Bobby. They both take bites out of their half.)

VIC THE BULLY: Really? Why do you have to be like that?

BOBBY: Because this cupcake is ours. And it's better to eat half a cupcake than none at all.

LOUIE: That's right!

VIC THE BULLY: You guys are no fun.

(Vic leaves.)

BOBBY: Nice job.

LOUIE: You too.

(They high five. Beat.)

BOBBY: You gonna eat the rest of yours?

(End of play.)

BAT, BIRDS, AND BEASTS
by Dominic Mishler

after Aesop's fable *Bat, Birds, and Beasts*

A long time ago, a feud broke out between the birds in the air and the beasts on the ground. No one is sure why, although various theories have been suggested. It's not important why the fighting started, only that it did.

The birds and the beasts had a mutual friend in Bat. He flew in the sky like a bird, but he had fur like a beast.

When the feud started, the beasts came to the Bat and asked him to take their side against the birds. The Bat was a beast. He had fur, not feathers like the birds. But Bat refused, saying he couldn't take sides. So the beasts went away.

The birds came to Bat and asked him to take their side against the beasts. He flew like a bird, he didn't walk on the ground like a beast. But Bat refused, saying he couldn't take sides. Soon, the fighting ended almost as quickly as it had started. Again, no one really knows why, and again, that is not important.

The birds and the beasts decided to have a party to celebrate the end of the feud. Bat noticed that he wasn't invited, so he invited himself and went to the party anyway. He asked why he wasn't invited; after all he hadn't taken sides in the fight. That was the problem, his former friends told him. He hadn't stood up for either of his friends.

If you try to be friends with everybody, you'll end up with no friends at all.

CAST OF CHARACTERS

DANI, female.
CHASE, male.
FIONA, female.

(It's not really a room, just an empty space under a set of stairs that the janitor forgets to lock. There are boxes and crates to sit on. DANI and CHASE enter and sit on the crates.)

DANI: She shouldn't have called you a thief.

CHASE: Of course Mrs. Douglas sided with her. Fiona's been every teacher's favorite since she tattled on people in preschool.

DANI: Chase—

CHASE: The principal called me in today. They're going to call my parents. I have to talk to the school psychiatrist tomorrow. I didn't even know we had a school psychiatrist.

DANI: Why?

CHASE: They think I'm a liar, everyone up at the office. They don't say it out loud. But they're using that slow, soft voice that means I'm guilty. They think I did it and if they're nice enough and patient enough I'll tell them.

DANI: You were the last one we know who had the money.

CHASE: I gave it to Mrs. Douglas.

DANI: You're saying Mrs. Douglas is lying?

CHASE: I don't know.

DANI: They really won't believe you if you say that.

CHASE: But it's the truth. They're going to call my parents. My parents won't believe me either. Especially after last year. You need to tell Mr. Peterson that I didn't do it.

DANI: But I know…

CHASE: Know what?

DANI: I know you were the last one with the money.

CHASE: But you're going to tell him I didn't take it, right? You promised to talk to him and tell him I was with you that afternoon.

DANI: But—

CHASE: I was with you.

DANI: Not all of it.

CHASE: Are you kidding me? Dani, you promised. I can get suspended if I can't prove I didn't do it.

DANI: Chase—

(FIONA enters.)

FIONA: Mr. Peterson called me out of class to his office. I have never been called out of class to the office ever. And it's because of you.

CHASE: No, I have a witness. Dani's going to tell Peterson that she was with me all afternoon.

FIONA: But she wasn't with you the whole time. She talked to me for like ten, twenty minutes when you took off right after school.

CHASE: I had to use the bathroom.

FIONA: TMI. Besides, she can't help you anyway. She agreed to be my witness. She said she would tell Peterson that I was with her when you were hiding the money. *(Pause while she figures it out:)* But if she tells Mr. Peterson she was with you, then it looks like I'm lying.

CHASE: *(To Dani:)* How can you be her witness and my witness?

FIONA: You were going to tell Mr. Peterson two different things?

CHASE: I can get suspended.

FIONA: So can I. Mr. Peterson thinks I know where the money is and that I'm covering for Chase. He thinks I helped him steal the gaming club's money. This has never happened to me before. I never even got detention till you people.

CHASE: Why would—

FIONA: Because I thought you were my friend. I picked you to be treasurer when Lisa moved. I trusted you and now they think I helped you.

CHASE: *(To Dani:)* Did you really tell Fiona that you'd say that?

FIONA: If you're going to be my witness, why did you say you'd tell Mr. Peterson he didn't do it?

CHASE: You lied. You lied to both of us.

DANI: I didn't lie.

FIONA: You promised to do things that you knew you wouldn't do.

CHASE: Sounds like lying to me.

DANI: I wasn't lying. I just couldn't pick one of you.

CHASE: I thought I was your best friend.

FIONA: I thought I was.

DANI: You both are.

CHASE: You can't do that. That's cheating.

FIONA: And you'd know all about that, wouldn't you?

DANI: That was low.

CHASE: *(To Dani:)* Stay out of this.

FIONA: Besides, it's true. He cheated on that test in math last year. But I stood up for you. I convinced the club to give you another chance. But you haven't changed.

CHASE: And how would you know? It's not like you're hanging out with us anymore.

FIONA: I really don't wanna have that fight again.

CHASE: Why don't you go hang out with your new friends over in the quad?

FIONA: Because they're not about to get me suspended for helping a thief.

DANI: I thought it was the right thing to do.

CHASE: So all three of us can get in trouble? Was that your plan? We could all spend our suspension together?

DANI: That was not my plan at all. My plans are better than that.

FIONA: Which one is it, Dani? Whose witness are you going to be?

DANI: Do I have to?

CHASE AND FIONA: Yes.

DANI: You two are the only friends I have.

FIONA: You'll end up with no friends at all.

(End of scene.)

(Lights up on the same space the next day. Dani is sitting alone. Chase and Fiona enter.)

DANI: Where have you been?

CHASE: Mr. Peterson called us into his office today. This morning, out of English. Mrs. Douglas was there with him. I thought this was it.

FIONA: But it was to tell us that Mrs. Douglas found the money. So nobody gets suspended.

CHASE: And they're going to call my parents, tell them about the mix up.

FIONA: So it's over.

DANI: Good.

CHASE: I told you I didn't steal it.

FIONA: The only proof you had was Dani. And I think we know how much that means.

CHASE: I'm innocent until proven guilty. Not that she was a big help.

DANI: If I had picked one over the other, one of you would have hated me.

CHASE: Now we both hate you.

FIONA: No we don't.

CHASE: What? I do. She was disloyal when I needed her.

FIONA: Your dad is letting you watch way too many war movies.

CHASE: Come on, you're not angry?

FIONA: Of course I'm angry.

CHASE: Not as angry as you were yesterday.

DANI: It's over, Chase.

CHASE: For you.

DANI: I did the right thing.

CHASE: You didn't do anything. That's the problem.

DANI: Nothing was the right thing.

CHASE: You could have ended it.

DANI: He wouldn't have believed me either.

FIONA: Especially when you told him two different stories.

DANI: I was in way over my head with this. I panicked. We all panicked.

CHASE: But you're the calm one, the smart one. That's why we needed you for this.

FIONA: That's why we both came to you.

DANI: Guys, I'm here now.

CHASE: When we don't need you anymore.

(Chase exits first, Fiona just after.)

DANI: But I need you.

(End of play.)

THE WARRIOR'S BELT
by Samantha Macher

after Aesop's fable *The Boy and the Nettles*

CAST OF CHARACTERS

MIGUEL, a boy.

LILI, his sister.

SENSEI, Miguel's Sensei.

Note: The opening Sensei monologue is optional and can be removed based on the intention of the performance (e.g. if the audience is intended to guess which fable it belongs to, etc.). It can also be moved to the end of the piece if needed.

SENSEI: A boy and his nettles: A Boy was stung by a Nettle. He ran home and told his Mother, saying, "What gives? Why does this hurt so bad? I barely touched the stupid nettle!!" Looking at him, exhaustedly, she asked, "Why the heck are you running around grabbing nettles?" She shook her long-suffering head. The boy shrugged, because he didn't *really* know. "Fine." She said. "Since it seems like you're going to do it anyway, next time you feel the need to touch a nettle, you have to grab it. Hard. Then, it won't sting you." Immediately after she finished her sentence, the boy ran outside and tried it again. He grabbed the nettle as hard as he could, and it did not sting him. *The moral? Whatever you do, do it with all your might.*

> *(A boy, MIGUEL, is hoping to get his [yellow] belt soon. He is practicing kata [combined fighting movements] for his upcoming test. His Sensei looks on exhausted.)*

MIGUEL: HIIIIIYA! *(He kicks:)* HIIIIIYA! *(He punches:)* HIYA! HIYA! HIYA! *(He does a variety of ill-coordinated movements:)* KWAAAAAAA—YAH! *(He does a poor imitation of a high kick:)* SCHWAAAA! *(He bows:)* Well?

SENSEI: Well, what?

MIGUEL: How was it?

SENSEI: Better than last week, I guess.

MIGUEL: Really?

SENSEI: You gotta ask?

MIGUEL: Yeah? How'd I look?

SENSEI: Geeze. Um. Uh. I don't know, how to tell you this, Miguel, but—

MIGUEL: What?

(His Sensei gives him a big thumbs-down.)

Seriously, bro?

SENSEI: I'm not your bro. I'm your Sensei. And I'm totally serious.

MIGUEL: But I did the—

(He makes a grasshopper pose.)

SENSEI: I saw that.

MIGUEL: And I went HIYA!

(He kicks.)

SENSEI: Yeah. So?

MIGUEL: So? Doesn't that count for anything?

SENSEI: Sure. You're, uh, burning calories, or getting your angries out, or something.

MIGUEL: I mean, for my belt.

SENSEI: Oh heck no.

MIGUEL: Why not?!

SENSEI: Karate is a sport of discipline, not just enthusiasm. Right now, you're pretty much just wiggling around. I don't know how to grade that—

MIGUEL: What can I do?

SENSEI: You've gotta look inside, kid. You have to find what centers you and then trust it. You have to find your warrior place. Calm your mind. It's the only way you'll get any better.

MIGUEL: Calm my mind? CALM MY MIND?! I'M ONLY A KID! My warrior place is where I play video games after eating a mountain of pixie sticks. This is the advice you're giving me?

SENSEI: I'm your Sensei, not your bosom friend. The only thing I can help you do is pass your test. Speaking of which, have you gotten over that last match—

MIGUEL: I don't want to talk about it.

SENSEI: Because if you're still hung up on what happened last time—

(Suddenly, the lights dim. Miguel is faced with a formidable opponent. LILI. Who has pigtails and a grimacing expression.)

LILI: HIYAAA!

(Lili punches Miguel right in the chest and he falls backward in slow motion. The lights come back up. Lili is gone.)

MIGUEL: I'm not hung up on anything.

SENSEI: But let's say you actually, secretly, kinda are, because you kinda are, there's no reason to be. Everyone gets their butt kicked by a girl at least once in their life.

MIGUEL: I did not get my butt kicked.

SENSEI: I got my butt kicked plenty of times. My cousin Sophie's the size of a linebacker and when I read her diary that day in the sixth grade, sheesh. That was a rough afternoon. Besides that twin sister of yours, Lili, well she's no softie—

MIGUEL: I did NOT get my butt kicked.

SENSEI: You should ask her where she found *her* warrior place.

MIGUEL: I did NOT get my butt kicked.

SENSEI: And hope it's genetic.

MIGUEL: I did NOT get—
GRRR!

SENSEI: —Tsk, tsk, tsk! All that— *(He flails:)* —ain't gonna cut it, Grasshopper.

(He exits.)

MIGUEL: Fine. FINE! Geeze. *(He calms himself:)* Focus. Work hard. Find your warrior place.

(He practices a few moves.)

Focus. Work hard. Find your warrior place.

(He tries a few more moves.)

Focus. Work hard. Find—

(Lili enters.)

LILI: Whatcha doin'?

MIGUEL: Not now. I'm practicing.

LILI: *(Earnestly:)* Are you practicing having a spasm?

MIGUEL: Zip it, Lili, I'm finding my warrior place.

LILI: Because if you're practicing karate, I think you might be doing it wrong.

MIGUEL: What do you know?

LILI: It should look more like this. *(She demonstrates perfect form:)* I can help you, if you want.

MIGUEL: No.

LILI: Are you sure, because I can—

MIGUEL: I said no!

(She looks shocked. Sad.)

I have to do it by myself. I have to find my warrior place.

LILI: Oh. Okay.

MIGUEL: And I can only do that in solitude.

LILI: Whatever you say.

(She starts to leave.)

MIGUEL: But, hey, Lili?

LILI: Yeah?

MIGUEL: If you could tell someone one thing, you know, hypothetically, to help them out, what would it be?

LILI: Um. I guess, I would probably tell them to try their best. No one who works hard ever fails.

MIGUEL: Did Sensei tell you that?

LILI: Sensei? No. He's crazy. Mom told me that last week before I took my spelling test.

MIGUEL: Was she right?

LILI: I got a "C."

MIGUEL: Not bad.

LILI: Yeah. I'm really more of a math gal.

(She exits. Miguel begins to practice his moves over and over, perhaps to the tune of a song like "Eye of the Tiger" alternating the mantras:)

MIGUEL: Focus. Work hard. Find your warrior place.

(And:)

No one who works hard ever fails.

(Suddenly, it's belt test day. A crowd of people are all around [this is probably the audience].)

SENSEI: Are you ready, Miguel?

MIGUEL: I think so.

SENSEI: Do you wish to meet your opponent?

MIGUEL: Do I have a choice?

SENSEI: Yeah. You can go home.

MIGUEL: Oh.

SENSEI: She's ready for you.

MIGUEL: *She?*

(Lili enters. She is prepared to battle.)

I can't fight *her again!* She's my sister and I just can't—

SENSEI: Hey, man. I'm your Sensei, not your family therapist. Now get on the mat and prepare to fight your twin sibling to the death.

MIGUEL: To the *death?*

SENSEI: Figure of speech, dude. You know what I mean.

LILI: Hey, bro.

MIGUEL: Lili, I don't think—

LILI: I can handle it.

MIGUEL: *(To himself:)* It's not her I'm worried about.

(The fight begins. The siblings engage one another. They both fight very respectably and for an entertaining duration of time, with a suitable amount of "HIYAs!" When the battle is concluded, Lili emerges again as the victor. Miguel looks utterly defeated, and not just because he has been utterly defeated. Lili goes over to Miguel.)

LILI: Good job out there.

MIGUEL: Thanks.

LILI: I can tell you worked really hard.

(The Sensei approaches.)

SENSEI: Yes. You did. *(He hands them both a yellow belt:)* And because of your effort, your diligence, and your courage to fight your most formidable opponent—

LILI: That would be me—

SENSEI: I have decided to award you your yellow belt.

MIGUEL: I got my belt?

SENSEI: Yeah. You both did. Nice work out there, you two.

(He exits.)

MIGUEL: Wow.

LILI: Congratulations. That was really great.

MIGUEL: Thanks.

(She hugs him. He recoils a little, and then leans into it.)

LILI: I'm gonna go tell Mom!

(She gets up and runs offstage.)

MIGUEL: Wait! I wanted to tell Mom! Lili! Wait up!

(He follows behind her. End of play.)

The Author Speaks
with Nicole B. Adkins, project leader for **Aesop Refabled**

What inspired you to write this play?
As the Youth Playwright-in-Residence/Youth Program Director at SkyPilot Theatre Company, I have been given the fantastic opportunity to create our programming for youth from scratch. For our first project, I wanted to employ our company's strengths, as well as answer what I saw as a wider need in the community. I have noticed that there seems to be a general lack of high quality professional theatre performances specifically designed for pre-teen and middle school students. So—I thought, hey! Let's get our writers on this. Though it was initially developed for professional touring for our theatre, we soon realized that *Aesop Refabled* could also be easily used in a classroom or "young actors" setting.

Was the structure of the play influenced by any other work?
There is a production model that the SkyPilot's Playwrights Wing regularly revisits: writing individual collections of short plays centered on a common theme. *Aesop Refabled* applied that technique to the challenge of adapting Aesop's classic fables for a modern audience.

What writers have had the most profound effect on your style?
Being a voracious reader, my style has developed under the influence of countless authors, though I suppose I can cite a few particular works that have greatly helped to shape my world-view and writing. Most notably, as a child I read every fairy-tale, collection of myths, and fantasy/science fiction novel I could get my hands on. I also loved historical fiction. Probably nearly all of my plays reflect these genre fascinations

to some degree—even if it is only to re-think an old concept—like a classic fable by Aesop! Some specific works (plays and novels) that have sunk into my bones include: everything by Hans Christian Anderson, *D'Aulaires' Book of Greek Myths*, *East of Eden* by John Steinbeck, *The Light Princess* by George MacDonald, *Ender's Game* by Orson Scott Card, ***The Yellow Boat*** by David Saar, ***The Commedia Princess and the Pea*** by Lane Riosley and Rebecca Byers, ***Little Medea*** by Melissa Cooper, and Shakespeare, because of the summer I spent studying his work in London, and because of the Shakespeare in the Park I did as a middle school student.

What are the most common mistakes that occur in productions of your work?
From time to time I have seen producers approach everything literally, without looking for ways to enhance the work with their own discoveries. A play is a blueprint—a picture in black and white that is waiting to have its colors filled in by the technicians and actors, and then brought into its third dimension through audience experience. The producing company should look for imaginative ways to achieve "stage magic" and to attain authenticity in interpreting the characters. *HOWEVER*, the other type of mistake that I have seen with my plays, and with the production of new plays in general, is when a producing company does not fully do their homework. It's important know the play through and through, work to puzzle/decipher/research the author's intent, and what may have influenced the writing of that particular work (perhaps mythology, or history, or references to topical events, etc). Each member of a producing company should always dive into the world of the play and try to articulate what, at its core, the play is really about. When they do that, then every decision can be made confidently, because it arises out of the play itself, and not from some

superimposed vision that has nothing to do with the actual heart of the play.

What inspired you to become a playwright?
I have acted in theatre since I was four years old, continuing since as a writer, actor, teacher, set painter, director, etc. I have seen time and time again how affecting theatre can be — for its participants and for its audience. I have also been smitten with writing and reading since I was seven. These areas of interest have merged naturally over the years... I think I've always been a playwright. As to pursuing it professionally, I dream one day of seeing original theatre for youth being as popular as books or movies — I mean, why not? It offers a completely different experience! I also think that this means youth must have plays that are as fresh, exciting, and dangerous — in other words, as cogent, as the plays offered to adult audiences. I think everyone deserves theatre at its best. That is my aim as a writer and theatre-maker — to make exciting theatre for youth, encourage other writers to do the same, and to be a part of the larger movement and discussion.

Shakespeare gave advice to the players in *Hamlet*; if you could give advice to your cast what would it be?
Explore the range of emotions in every character. I'm a big fan of finding the humor, and the tragedy in moments — especially the "180." I think one of the most amazing things in the world is to watch people's quick realizations — to see them instantly (and authentically) change their mind, demeanor, and/or objective. I think humor and tragedy can be found in unexpected places. Figure out what your character really wants, and let every decision arise from that pursuit.

How was the first production different from the vision that you created in your mind?
I don't know that I am one to have particular expectations. I always long to be surprised (and hopefully delighted) by what actors and technicians bring to the table. Our director made the decision to bridge the transition between each play with the moral from the original fable that inspired the piece. I thought that was a strong choice. It inspired our playwrights to write an individually rewritten version of each fable and moral that we could include in the published edition of this collection, for the flexible use of any production company! This was a great example of how a production of a new work can enhance the long-term life of its script.

About the Authors

SkyPilot Theatre Company is a Los Angeles-based ensemble of theatre artists, founded in 2006 by artistic director Bob Rusch, and dedicated to developing new plays from conception through production in world premiere stagings. The Playwrights Wing is SkyPilot's resident team of professional writers, composers and lyricists tasked with creating original material for collaboratively-written projects, such as *Aesop Refabled*, featuring the company's corps of resident actors, while developing their own individual work through SkyPilot's signature New Plays Workshop. Visit SkyPilot on the web at: www.skypilottheatre.com. The authors of *Aesop Refabled* are playwrights-in-residence Nicole B. Adkins, Jeff Goode, Adam Hahn, Samantha Macher, Liz Shannon Miller, Dominic Mishler, Mike Rothschild and Dave Ulrich.

About YouthPLAYS

YouthPLAYS (www.youthplays.com) is a publisher of award-winning professional dramatists and talented new discoveries, each with an original theatrical voice, and all dedicated to expanding the vocabulary of theatre for young actors and audiences. On our website you'll find one-act and full-length plays and musicals for teen and pre-teen (and even college) actors, as well as duets and monologues for competition. Many of our authors' works have been widely produced at high schools and middle schools, youth theatres and other TYA companies, both amateur and professional, as well as at elementary schools, camps, churches and other institutions serving young audiences and/or actors worldwide. Most are intended for performance by young people, while some are intended for adult actors performing for young audiences.

YouthPLAYS was co-founded by professional playwrights Jonathan Dorf and Ed Shockley. It began merely as an additional outlet to market their own works, which included a substantial body of award-winning published and unpublished plays and musicals. Those interested in their published plays were directed to the respective publishers' websites, and unpublished plays were made available in electronic form. But when they saw the desperate need for material for young actors and audiences—coupled with their experience that numerous quality plays for young people weren't finding a home—they made the decision to represent the work of other playwrights as well. Dozens and dozens of authors are now members of the YouthPLAYS family, with scripts available both electronically and in traditional acting editions. We continue to grow as we look for exciting and challenging plays and musicals for young actors and audiences.

About ProduceaPlay.com

Let's put up a play! Great idea! But producing a play takes time, energy and knowledge. While finding the necessary time and energy is up to you, ProduceaPlay.com is a website designed to assist you with that third element: knowledge.

Created by YouthPLAYS' co-founders, Jonathan Dorf and Ed Shockley, ProduceaPlay.com serves as a resource for producers at all levels as it addresses the many facets of production. As Dorf and Shockley speak from their years of experience (as playwrights, producers, directors and more), they are joined by a group of award-winning theatre professionals and experienced teachers from the world of academic theatre, all making their expertise available for free in the hope of helping this and future generations of producers, whether it's at the school or university level, or in community or professional theatres.

The site is organized into a series of major topics, each of which has its own page that delves into the subject in detail, offering suggestions and links for further information. For example, Publicity covers everything from Publicizing Auditions to How to Use Social Media to Posters to whether it's worth hiring a publicist. Casting details Where to Find the Actors, How to Evaluate a Resume, Callbacks and even Dealing with Problem Actors. You'll find guidance on your Production Timeline, The Theater Space, Picking a Play, Budget, Contracts, Rehearsing the Play, The Program, House Management, Backstage, and many other important subjects.

The site is constantly under construction, so visit often for the latest insights on play producing, and let it help make your play production dreams a reality.

More from YouthPLAYS

Herby Alice Counts Down to Yesterday by Nicole B. Adkins
Comedy. 45-50 minutes. 3-7 males, 3-7 females, 4-20+ either (10-50+ performers possible).

Middle school rocket scientist Herby Alice has ambitions as big as the universe, and no time for interviews. Rose Plum, media hopeful, needs a juicy story to get in good with the school broadcast elite. How far is she willing to go to be a star? Or will mad scientists, aliens, befuddled teachers, demanding executives, and the space-time continuum overrun the show?

Harry's Hotter at Twilight by Jonathan Dorf
Comedy. 90-100 minutes. 5-25+ males, 7-25+ females (12-50+ performers possible).

In this crazed mash-up parody of *Harry Potter* and *Twilight*—with cameos crashing in from *Lord of the Rings*, *Star Wars*, *Alice in Wonderland* and many other places—you'll encounter deli-owning vegetarians, invisible rabbits, magical carrot weapons, random lunatics, soothing offstage voices, evil gourmets and much more, as everyone's favorite wizards, vampires and werewolves battle to save miserable, gloomy Spork—and indeed the world—from certain destruction.

The Old New Kid by Adam J. Goldberg
Comedy. 30-40 minutes. 2-9+ males, 3-10+ females (8-30+ performers possible).

It's the half-day of school before Thanksgiving break, and current "new kid" Alan Socrates Bama just wants to get through the day. But when a new-new kid arrives, things change. Alan has three hours to find the meaning of Thanksgiving, survive elementary school politics, battle for his identity, and spell the word "cornucopia" in this *Peanuts*-flavored comedy for kids of all ages.

Telling William Tell by Evan Guilford-Blake
Dramedy. 80-85 minutes. 7-11 males, 4-10 females (11-21 performers possible).

The children grab the spotlight in this retelling of the story of the mythical Swiss hero—famed for shooting an apple off his son's head—framed by a fictionalized story of Rossini writing his famed opera. Music by the great composer enriches this thrilling tale of Switzerland's fight for freedom and the birth of a new work of musical art.

Secret Life Under the Stairs by Kris Knutsen
Dramedy. 30-35 minutes. 2 males, 2 females.

Nothing much seems to happen in the isolated town of Echo, Nevada...that is until a new kid shows up and disturbs the secret hideout of a group of not-so-friendly misfits. Lu, Bizzy, and twins Catch and Field spend an afternoon discovering things they never knew about friendship, trust, and a mysterious and disgusting "Death Jar." A play about making friends, navigating change, and exploring imaginative worlds that are often lurking under the stairs.

The Jungle Book by Callan Stout
Adventure. 70-75 minutes. 6-22 males, 2-8 females (7-24 performers possible).

In this adaptation of Kipling's famous stories, the beat of a drum and the cry of a wolf give way to the sounds of ferocious tiger Shere Khan on the hunt. But when the wolf pack discovers that he is hunting a human child, they rescue the infant Mowgli from the tiger's teeth. Mother and Father Wolf adopt the man-cub, and with the protection of Bagheera the panther and the teachings of Baloo the bear, Mowgli lives peacefully with the wolves. But as he grows into manhood, he will not be able to escape his inevitable showdown with Shere Khan.

The Unscary Ghost by Matt Buchanan
Comedy. 40-50 minutes. 3+ males, 5+ females, 8+ either (13-30+ performers possible).

Loosely based on Oscar Wilde's *The Canterville Ghost*. When the Otis family moves into the old Victorian home in Canterville, Ohio, they soon learn that the place is haunted—by a ghost who can't scare anyone. The jaded, modern family alternately taunts and tries to exploit the unfortunate ghost, Simon Canter, even trying to get a spot on the hit TV show, *America's Most Haunted*. Only the oldest daughter, Ginny, seems to care for or understand poor Simon. Can she help him find peace? A sometimes zany, sometimes touching show for the whole family.

Welcome to the Neighborhood by Steven Stack
Suspense. 25-35 minutes. 1 male, 5 females, 4-12 either (10-22 performers possible).

Chloe is the new girl in Shadow Oaks, a neighborhood where things are not what they seem. As she attends her first slumber party with her new friends, what begins innocently enough slowly gives way to a chilling standoff as Chloe faces a decision that will define her for the rest of her life in this allegory about the pressures teens face to conform.

Robin Hood and the Heroes of Sherwood Forest by Randy Wyatt
Adventure. 60-70 minutes. 9-30 males, 6-24 females (18-40+ performers possible).

This fresh adaptation of the classic English tale emphasizes a community of heroes as Robin Hood and his friends band together to save the poor people of Nottingham from unjust taxation and poverty at the hands of Prince John and his longsuffering yet cruel Sheriff. Two gypsy orphans, Maid Marion's handmaiden and a mysterious stranger share a secret that could win the day—or see Robin hanged by morning!

Made in the USA
Middletown, DE
24 November 2018